Recharge Your Spirit

echoes of a shepherd

Mark A. Norris

PublishAmerica
Baltimore

ISBN: 1-4241-6208-4
PUBLISHED BY PUBLISHAMERICA, LLLP
www.publishamerica.com
Baltimore

Printed in the United States of America

About the Author

Mark Norris, a born-again inspirational speaker, who has talked across Canada on, Harmony with Nature and Spiritual Peace. Mark believes that we all share a bond with creation, that true health, true beauty, starts from within. He writes with care and passion to help one to the world.

Dedicational

For the glory of the one who guided my words on top of that mountain. For the message that I heard contained within the song, sung by a little bird. My father in heaven, our great Creator, Almighty God.

To the one who has always encouraged my dreams, my sweet Tanya, and my son for daily teachings, and all the fun

To my Mother, who started me on this path I walk, and for so much more, to good ol' Opa, for all our talks on history

To my brother Kevin, for many spiritual gifts, and the keen sense of direction, to his wife Janet, a good heart

To my brother David, for the love of NASCAR and sports, for all my memories, to his son Tyler, and wife Cheryl

To my sister Deborah, for the love of horses, and country roads, to her sons Shawn and Nathan

To Myra, a fun and cool mother n law, who makes great lasagna, to Jimmie James a true mountain man, to Kelsey Rae Dawn a beautiful name. To Darryl, for all our NFL Sundays.

For my sweetie rottwieller Tia, for all our adventures
and unconditional love, "I miss you girl"

To Mark T, Tim T, Mike P, Todd, Pat, Paul,
Jeff G, Mike L, and all my friends,

To all of you that may read,

To all that I have encountered in life,

I thank you all, God bless and journey well in life...

Acknowledgments

To all of you at PublishAmerica, for caring about the world and final touch on my dream

To Sid Oliveira, of After Hours Computing Services, in Kingsville, Ontario for your willingness to help another

To Kevin and Candace of Sure Copy in Kamloops, BC for your kindness and touch on my manuscript

A Personal Note

Hello there, I am Mark Aaron Norris. For 40 years, or falling leaf seasons, I have seen the setting sun. I have seen the brightness of beyond and my eternal light is on. For today, tomorrow Recharge your Spirit, is a rising sun. Embrace its warm healing rays. We are here to be ourselves, to care for one another, to share our surroundings, to love.

Writing in nature, allows me to write from the teacher within. Touching deep beyond what is taken in by the eye. To the mind, and the spirit. A book that was written to inspire a healthier existence in everyway, everyday.

The key to peace lies within the spirit. If one spirit can touch another and another, eventually our little world will be a brighter place for all people. For you to the world I care, my wisdom to share, written with love to open the hearts door, and so much more.

Sing your song from your heart,

...for the future...

God bless and good journeys

"Sometimes a small ripple is all that is needed"

From Me to You

Together we are about to embark on a magical journey. A journey in poetic rhyme that is full of emotion, truth, and imagination. Yet, experienced through life, it will touch you in so many ways.

The following pages as you will find are not just your average poems. They are something more. I call my writing in this book, PoeArtry. They come with meaning, messages, that are different page by page, yet overall the same. Throughout my book, I sometimes refer to it as PoeArtry.

Never has a book captured a dreams essence, allow your mind to go through its metamorphosis, across the threshold of space and time, leaving the illusion behind, curl up, and let's begin...

All aboard...here we go...

Enemy

War going on everywhere, bombs bursting in the air,
Bullets ringing by, planes above, people dying everywhere,
Minutes seem like hours, to a young soldier, eyes of blue,
Remembering his training, he runs forward, straight and true.

Thinking of childhood games, back home, now breathing hard,
Dirty, hungry, and tired, from home, he seems so far,
A noise, he turns, he is eye to eye, with the enemy,
Both raise their guns in surprise, both very, jumpy.

Is this, now the end of life, both young, neither have had a wife,
Eye's locked, nervous fingers on each trigger, a single thought,
LIFE,
Different languages, both no words to say,
Both value life, and they will not die today.

Lowering their weapons, they turn and walk away,
The war ended, both returned home the next day,
Thirty years of peace, have now passed by,
The young soldier, a lawyer now, a family's love, in his eye.

Out for dinner, at his favorite eating place,
A family walks in, eyes lock, must be the fates,
Both stand, smile, cry, hug, shake hands and say,
Thank you so much for saving my life that day,

Great friends they came to be,
Where once they stood, as the enemy,
To this day, both, you can hear them say,
We wouldn't be here, if we had pulled the trigger, that day.

Little Bird

Little bird in a city, I wonder, what you may see,
Ruffling of feathers, stirred awake, by the buzz of a bee,
A little bird takes flight, for a morning meal, to fly,
See's a man, yelling at his wife and child, as he takes to the sky.

Over a roof, there is a girl, putting something in her arm,
Over another, two boys, playing catch, like on a farm.
Over another, a man, is taking his own precious life,
One more, he lands on a balcony, a husband leaving a child and wife.

"I'm off to work, my love," he kisses, both as he goes,
Having breakfast, saying grace, love, this family knows.
The little bird is off again, sirens sound in the air,
"Someone's been shot," the bird hears, "This isn't fair.

Flying now, in the direction of the park,
A dog tied to a tree, beaten and painted, left there since dark.
Midday in the park, a stabbing for a wallet, a man runs away,
A homeless man, for food, being turned away.

The little bird, returns to a tree, and disappears,
Above the stars in the sky, he reappears.
Beside another, he hears and angelic voice say,
Lord Jesus, why the tear in your eye, today.

First Base

"It's starting to rain Willy," but Willy was determined, somehow,
"C'mon, one more try Dad, "Ok, let's go, it's really coming down now.
Picking up his son, both laughing, running to the car,
On the way home, Willy, noticed people, walking in and out of a bar.

"This Saturday, I'm going to get to first base, Dad," feeling great,
Little Willy, was on a baseball team, you see, at age eight.
The week passed by, Willy's day had finally came,
He stepped up to the plate, when the coach, called his name.

Dad looks intense, he concentrated, he swung strike one,
"That's my boy, good try son," Dad said, as he swung, this time it rung.
One foot in front of the other, he made it to first base,
Dad, a tear in his eye, yesterday a judge, heard a three year old case.

About how a drunk driver, had taken a life,
A woman, a mother, someone's loving wife.
Another victim, a boy, lost both legs to prosthetic limbs,
    drunk driver don't you see,
That little Willy, that little boy, is now a war amputee.

The ball, was carried on Angels wings, that day,
Willy had hit a home run, step by step, he made it all the way.
Sitting on a cloud, and angel smiles,
Dad and son, talked about the homerun, for quite a while.

A Ripple

Recharge you Spirit is a ripple, in the big pond of life,
Where do you think the ripple will go? I ask my wife.
To one like you I'd send it, to one who dared to dream,
They will help you get it to the world, so it may be seen.

From one to many, I hope my ripple will touch,
A treasure amongst books, it will be treated as such.
Over land, over water, through air, the ripple will be heard,
A ripple, that, is carried, within the song of a bird.

This ripple will it travel fast or slow,
The answer, myself, I don not know.
For this, I have asked for help, from another,
Like this book, there is no other.

The ripple will it even be felt by one or more,
I believe in my dream, it will help some, open a door.
The ripple may be felt by a husband and wife,
I pray the ripple will help many in life.

The ripple may help some, see in a different way,
What they have been missing in life, until today.
The ripple, I have created in a unique way,
To spread the message, share love, and kindness, everyday.

The Letter

Two young people in love, spring 1940, high school sweethearts,
Best friends in youth, as adults, in love from the start.
Plans for their wedding and future, they make,
Sitting with family, talking, sharing tea and cake.

The mailman has come, the young man, has been drafted today,
Hitler is in Europe, he bombed London, today,
"I love you, I'll be back, I'll find a way," were his last works to say,
She waves goodbye, to his ship, leaving the bay.

Bye's are short, now given a gun, grenades, and a uniform,
"History, is made today," he hears their mission,
a beach, they will storm,
It's early in the morning, he can see his breath, in the morning frost,
Bombs, bullets, panic everywhere, innocent lives being lost.

She awaits his return, safely some day,
A year has passed, she gets a visit, from the Army today,
Told the news, how the young man had died a Hero that day,
Sad, yet proud, as she knew, he would not have it, any other way.

Decades pass, the war, a long time over,
Married, kids, a career, she is now much older,
The mailman has come, a letter for you Mom, she hears,
She looks at it, swept up by emotion, followed by tears.

It's from the young man, so long ago, so many years,
Finally it reaches her, alone now, with dried tears,
She opens the letter, begins to read and cry,
"My Darling, where do I start, you are the twinkle in my eye,
I Love you with all my heart, I have from the start, and I will beyond,
It's crazy over here, we storm a beach tomorrow, at dawn,
My love, if you get this letter, and I by chance do not live on,
If I do not return, promise me, to live on, for me, my love,
I will always be with you, just from above,
So many good memories, that we share,
I miss you so much, for you, I care
I love you my Darling.

She whisper's back, "I love you"
She closes her eyes, remembering their love so true,
So long, the letter, how did it find her, reach her, this is the mystery,
Holding the letter close to her heart, thoughts of their special history.

The Deer

Waking up in a field, surrounded by wildflowers,
Clouds to the west, it may bring showers,
I have a full rack of antlers, this year,
Last year no chance, to be with, a female deer.

Six points I have, a strong buck, I have become,
Any challenge, in the rut, this time, I'll overcome,
I have lived through a tornado, and a forest fire,
I nearly escaped that day, a car blew a tire.

The woods today are alive, as I make my rounds,
The birds, talking in their language, what beautiful sounds,
I am thirsty, to my drinking place, I will go,
I am happy, across the stream, another buck, it's my bro,

We talk of Mom, and days, when we were just fawns,
Laughed, had dinner, he had to go, just before dawn,
I love these woods, this is my place to be,
Such peace and beauty, I wish all could see.

Today I feel to stretch my 4 legs, and go for a run,
To my meadow I go, surrounded by wildflowers, under the sun,
A beautiful day, the sky is so blue, clouds so white,
Great run, time to stop and have a little bite.

BAM! The pain, all through me, down I have to lay,
What's happening, I feel myself fading away,
My dying breath, Humans, I cannot believe, what they say,
"My head will look good on the wall," for this I die, today.

Elevator Disease

Spreading everywhere, the Elevator Disease,
No cure found, it's all over these days,
It affects us all, transmitted how, they do not know,
All around us, even if you go to a show.

It's with us, when we have to stand in line,
It's with us, everywhere, all the time,
A simple hello, how are you, taken away,
Standing there, voiceless shells, of who we are,
at that moment of the day,

You'll see if you have it now, you'll become aware,
Surrounded by other people, you just stand, and stare,
What is everyone looking at, when nothing is there,
It makes for a cold world, of the Elevator Disease, Beware.

I think what the cure can be found,
When you are with others, on common ground,
A simple, "Hello, Good day to you."
This is the cure, I believe to be true.

Invisible

Two days till Christmas, unnoticed, keeps to himself,
Walks into a store for warmth, pretending to look
    for some item on the shelf,
On a mission to a church, for a hot meal,
A hot meal, warm building, a sermon and a prayer, what a deal.

It's nighttime soon, people passing him by,
Not one hello, or a meeting of the eye,
Sinking deeper within, before this, he had lost,
His wife and child, he is starting to feel the frost.

Cheeks numb, feet freezing, his will, all but stolen away,
None offer kindness to him, he realizes, he has become invisible today,
Trying to find shelter, he sees Christmas lights,
Remembering, days of old, when life was so bright.

It's very cold now, -30 now, for a coffee, he is turned away,
Looks a mess, customers, look and no words to say,
He's back, searching for shelter on the street,
Freezing cold, crying, "Why, has this happened to me"
    he can't feel his feet,

He finds a place, to his knees, before sleep, he always prays,
"God bless all, grant peace, love, to all in need, Amen,"
    was all he had to say
Shivering and shaking, he tried to go to sleep, way too cold,
He begins to dream, of the days of old.

Two days after Christmas now, he is found,
Curled up, and frozen to the ground,
A smile from ear to ear,
On a warm beach, with his kid, he fears, "Let's go for a walk my dear"

I just had a nightmarish dream, all he could say,
"LIFE IS THE DREAM, HEAVEN IS REAL," he heard someone say,
An Angel stood before him," LOVE YOU ALL," the angel, took flight,
Together again, he realized, Heaven is bright.

Bully

Bully, you are blind, and cannot see,
For the victim, the future outcome may be,
Thinking parents, no time, or understanding,
Of school life, peer- pressure, too demanding.

Afraid to confront, because of fear,
For a bullied child, we should shed a tear,
A bully, a friend with one, who would be,
Not much of a future, can't you see.

Maybe jail, or end up on cops,
Definitely not proud, all your Grand pops,
After school, a bully, all alone,
Renting a room, in a basement, in someone else's home.

Applying for a job, now 24, the bully, searching now for something more,
The bully, a unionized factory, the interviewer, the victim,
     opens the door,
Parents raised me to pay attention in school,
Few times you were cool, by beating me up, now who is the fool.

To hold a grudge, after reading, Recharge your Spirit, is not for me,
A better person, for this, I will be,
You have the job, you start on Monday,
To help peace on earth, in my own small way.

Thinking back on how he could have gone to school, with a _____,
Decided instead, to hit the books, become as bright as the sun,
If he had he would have missed out on all the fun,
Like this football game, with his wife, watching their son.

So happy now, 3 bedroom home, 2 car garage,
A life that, back then, seemed only like a mirage,
Florida vacation, all the toys, that anyone would need,
Thanks to Recharge your Spirit, he did not let the bully win,
and take seed.

Turn a negative into a positive,
It's not worth it, being destructive,
Turn it around, be creative,
Your in control, of you, be constructive.

You may be happy, with what the outcome may be,
Even if right now, you cannot see,
For the future and what it may bring,
Take hold of your future, Let it sing.

Years ago, I bought a book, at a bookstore,
Recharge your Spirit, changed my life, helped me open a door,
So much sense, this book meant to me,
It helped me be, the man in the mirror, the man I see.

The Mirror

Reflections in a mirror, reflections past, reflection back,
Look at what is looking back, in ones life, reflections stack,
Looking back with reflections eyes, beyond the surface, look deep,
Within, to the center, to the beauty within, yes, even after sleep.

From the beginning of time, for surface beauty,
    the mirror has been used,
About their own self beauty, it has made some confused,
For only the surface, the mirror reflects,
Looking within the eyes of eyes, one's inner self can detect.

Next time, you are at a mirror, look deep within the eyes,
Looking to see, what others may possibly pass by,
To who you are, and see what you see,
Dare to dream, and be who you are to be.

My Best Friend

A cowboy like me, best friends, by fate, our destiny,
In times of trouble, you are always there for me,
We've been through so much together, in our history,
Why we are best friends, is not a mystery,
My best friend will lift me up, when I am down,
They'll help me smile, when on my face is a frown,
My best friend, you will always be,
Some decisions, the right choice, you help me see.

Whether in a car, or on a hike, no matter the weather,
Together on a trail we found a eagle feather,
You and I, so many memories that we share,
There is no doubt, that for me, you care,
You are always with me in my heart,
Even when I'm creating, my work of art,
My best friend, your as true as glue,
Without you, I do not know what I would do.

We jam to music, have fun, and just pal around,
Your always so dependable, when I need you, you can be found,
You are best friends, forever, with me,
You see my best friend, you see, no other it can be, it's me,
You must love yourself, before you can love another,
So true to myself, a friendship like no other,
With yourself, a best friend you should be,
Believing in you and your dreams,
A best friend will help you see,
That your dreams may come to be.

Peace, Earth Race

Sharing this planet, God created for us, Earth for free,
We all breathe the same air,
About something, we all care,
We look at the same sun and moon,
Differences apart, we pull together, in trouble like a typhoon,
Individuals, with many a different face,
Sharing this planet, we are the Earth race.

Color, language, it does not matter,
We are all humans, our hearts, all the same, pitter patter,
Water binds us all, and makes us who we are,
Not from other worlds, just a country, really not that far,
Casualties, we all feel the loss of war,
Building weapons of mass destruction, when have we gone too far,
Fighting amongst each other, since the beginning of time,
History, always a teacher, through father time,
When will we learn, from teachings like this rhyme
Progress seems to be our global concern, we must keep pace,
Sharing this planet, we are the Earth race.

Our goal should be, to make our world a better place,
Where all at peace, better for mankind, the whole, the race,
Doing good, showing kindness, wherever it is needed,
This is a message sent, a message to be heeded,
Hug a tree, be gentle with an animal,
Be a true friend, always so dependable,
To pass, what we live, into the future,
Let it be, peace, love, an admiration and respect of nature,

Let it be clean air, water, and so much more,
Let it be so, a world in harmony, for our children's, children, do this for,
Not bottles, cans, garbage, pollution, we will lose the race,
Too much negative, we won't be able to keep pace,
Sharing this planet, we are the Earth race

War, greed, starvation, crimes, a thing of the past,
Songbirds sing, do you hear their song at last?
Peace and tranquility, throughout the lands,
Dancing in the streets, to the music of street bands,
The rich, the poor, all willing to help, to love,
It's a beautiful day, sunlight reflects, off the wings of a white dove,
Blue sky, this enchanted day,
The earth, should have always been this way,
To the future we have learned, from history,
Time for a change, the Earth's fate, inevitably our destiny,
This is but one man's testimony,
Who set this pace, slow down as the turtle, and we'll win the race,
Sharing the planet, WE ARE THE EARTHRACE.

Decisions

Different paths, we take, choices that we make,
Life altering occurrences, every turn, so much at stake,
Take the time, to think it through, with precision,
The choice at hand, is yours to make, give it your full attention.

Roads we choose, in a blink of an eye,
May affect the rest of your life, until the day, you die,
Things change and do not stay the same,
No other at fault, the decision you made, is to blame.

Be careful about the decision, you make today
The result, you may or may not like, and it may be there to stay,
Be wise, like the Owl, look at things, from different angles
Some decisions aren't as easy as, Donut or Bagel.

The choices we make, the ripples we feel
Choices we make, success or fail,
Choices we make, may seem like fate
The choices we make, may be who to date.

Never be rushed, pressured, be you, and think of the results
In youth sometimes, the right decision, can make you more adult,
Choices to be made, to open what door
The decision made, I wonder, what's in store.

War

This thing, they named war, doesn't make much sense,
One country, a Christmas tree, with Christmas presents,
On TV, another country, bombs flashing, bullets ringing,
Histories mistakes, celebrations of peace on earth,
we should be singing.

Historic mistakes, over and over,
Why don't we learn, when we see, woman and children,
running for cover,
To this day, we arm and fight one another,
Sharing the planet, all our fates, are interwoven together.

Some solutions, can be found,
The World, all on common ground,
This thing they call war can anyone stop it,
Adults, just sit down and talk about it.

We've progressed so far, yet we have learned little,
When will anyone, War, solve the answer, to this riddle?
We have millions of dollars spent on destruction,
Yet all over, there are poor, dying of starvation.

When will it stop, hatred, racism, in another's eyes,
When will it stop, the loss of, too many innocent lives,
We teach our young, to learn from their mistakes,
Pages from our history, show us what it takes.

To put an end to war, forever and ever,
Peace on Earth, am I just a dreamer,
I think not, I think it can be,
If we could learn from our mistakes, from the pages of history.

Dream of a Dream

I have dreamed a dream, and this is what I see,
To dream this dream, a dreamer, I must be,
Will this dream I see, come to pass
Only myself, can I ask.

A dream of a dream, dreaming of PoeArtry
Where to begin, where do I start,
My talent, I'm sent, a mix of poetry and art,
Pen in hand, beginning of my dream, about to start.

My dream tells me, to write about experiences, about life,
That people will fell, surprised, not my wife,
My dream, a message overall, for one to all to hear,
Become awake, don't hibernate through life, as the bear.

My dream, I dream, now becoming a reality
PoeArtry, flowing through me, lessons, stories, and things of history,
Telling a story, a different angle in poetic rhyme,
PoeArtry, my dream, for the world, just in time.

In store now, Recharge your Spirit, a book, worth the look,
For this will be a favorite, for all who like books,
What it took was, writing with good intent with good meaning,
Dream, the dream, I dream, and to all of you, keep DREAMING.

PoeArtry

Poetic Art for the eyes, since the dawn of age
Poetic words swept away, with a turn of a page,
Sculptures, paintings, forever in our minds
Soft as a written word, forever in time.

Thinking from deep center, where within, all begins
Taken in by our eyes, touching your heart and spirit within,
It can help you fly, touching the sky, inspiring the day
PoeArtry, is an art form, once read, forever it will stay.

From the heart, comes the art of PoeArtry
Healing words, that fall in with destiny,
Angels on soft, white, fluffy clouds
You are drifting away, with each word, read aloud.

A written or spoken word, is a beautiful thing
Kind, peaceful, full of grace, never meant to sting,
Put together in a wondrous sentence
Bright as a Christmas tree, and presents.

Poetry and Art, forever, together they belong
In PoeArtry, written in word, may be a song,
If other's read, it as it was meant to share
PoeArtry, from the heart, show that we care.

A Dream

A thing of beauty, sometimes, maybe a foretelling, to be weary
Sometimes confusing, exciting, extraordinary,
Pictures, dancing in your mind, while your sleeping
Stirred, woken up, by the images, you were seeing.

Purple sky, 3 moons and a unicorn
People have been dreaming, dreams, since time was born,
Some say, there messages, what you see in a dream
What I just saw, what could that, possibly mean?

Flying like and eagle, above the mountains, so high
I'm in a submarine now, I hear, it's time, to dive,
Giant leather wings, I'm on the back of a dragon
Back to childhood now, pulling my cat, in my little red wagon.

I love dreaming, I can't wait, to do so, tonight
From space, Earth appears, so bright,
Maybe this time, I'll be superman
Or the lead singer, on stage, with my band.

They can mystify, scare, amaze, us all
You wake up quick, if you dream, you trip or fall,
What was going on, where were you, heading
Some crazy adventure, I am betting.

Some say, you may get, visits from the other side
Walking on a beach, drifting, with the change of the tide,
I believe that this may sometimes, be true
Just as sure as I am, that the sky is blue.

Dreams may be of the past, or of things yet to see
Dream a dream, for me to see, the winning numbers for the lottery,
This has yet, come to be
Because, dreams remain a mystery.

A part of us, our subconscious, while we sleep
Imagination, Spirit take over, in a sleep, that is deep,
No more gravity, to keep us grounded
What was that? An elephant just sounded.

Dream a dream, a dream weaver, you are
A Dream catcher, facing a bright star,
Peaceful sleep and dream of all the wonder, that you will see
In tonight's dreams, that come to be.

A New Day

Recharge your Spirit, a new day for me
Years wasted, all the time, not really being me,
Recharge your Spirit, by Mark Norris, has helped me see
To be me, and become the man, I will, in the future, be.

Shakespeare, Edgar Allan Poe, to Robert Frost
Without Mark Norris, as a writer, the world so much lost,
I owe it all to him, dreaming a dream
He helped me realize, how beautiful life can seem.

Within a page, a magical transformation
Between the lines, the rhyme, the lesson, the stories, what a creation,
Recharge your Spirit, written from one heart to another
Mark A Norris grabs you from the start, a writer like this, no other.

A writer, before his time, decades, future generations
Mark, a pen and paper, what a wondrous transformation,
A message sent, within, a message to change, and live by
Admiring so much beauty, I used to take for granted, with my eye.

Recharge you Spirit, helped me find faith, the Bible and God above
It helped me see, what life is to be, and found love,
Helped me with a decision, helped change me life
I continue the echoes, now I share it with me children and wife.

So if you're at a crossroad, and a book, you like to read
Pick up Recharge you Spirit, new things, new ideas, will take seed,
Inspiring, how one can relate, because the book is so true
To you Mark Norris, the world, but I, for one thank you.

Not yet famous, what, how can this be?
One of the greatest writers, in our history,
He should be on Oprah, Recharge your Spirit, on topic, on TV
She could help, Marks dream, a reality to be
To help one, two, or the world to see.

For such a short book, what meaning, it has such an impact
Recharge your Spirit you'll come to love and that's a fact,
It's a book you'll read over and over
It's a magical doorway, Recharge your Spirit, just open the cover.

A Name

What is in a name? Creations, like you and me
Without a name, who would we be?
A beautiful name that all can see
A name is something, given in life, that is free.

One of the most beautiful that I have ever heard
Sounds pleasing to my ears, like the song of a bird,
Kelsey-Rae Dawn, and angelic sounding name
It may be given to more than one, neither are the same.

Katrina-Lynn is another one, names, millions out there
Once a nice name heard, it stays, like a favorite song you hear,
A lifetime of memories, are found within, a person's name
There is no name, to be hidden in shame.

For every name, names on e of God's beautiful creations
For some names, invented for inventions,
But every name has come with good intentions
Some names are hard, causing a moments reflection.

Be happy with the name given to you
You are wondrous creation, this is true,
A name helps you be who you are
A famous name, if you are a star.

Be proud you are found, within a name
Original, even if another's name, the same,
Beauty, is found in a name
Looking in a mirror, your looking at a member of:
 the human, hall of fame.

A Shadow

What is in a shadow, where there is not light
It hides from us in areas that are bright,
On a hot day, the trees shadow, become a friend
Once in awhile, you check to be sure, back together again.

It has been there right from the start
Growing with us, yet it has no heart,
In one place, it can seem to be
On a walk, behind, then way in front of me.

By yourself, you are never alone
Even though it has no name, or no home,
A shadow is always with you
A friend, true as glue.

What becomes of the shadow, in the dark
Does it come within, then dreams begin, a walk in the park,
Why does the shadow, follow us all through life
It doesn't have a say in anything, like who I take, for a wife.

A silent life for a shadow, it must be
I wonder if the shadow, even knows of me, or can it see?
As I write this my shadow, a pen, it is with me
Faithful shadow, he'd rather be with me, than be free.

A Fallen Cloud

Clouds, effortlessly, they move and dance with the wind
Different sizes and shapes, for a child's imaginative whim,
On a sunny warm day, they can bring to us, shade
Day of overcast," I'm sure, my sun bill paid."

In time of drought, they can bring to us, rain
Nothing quite like dancing, or playing in the rain,
Clouds so bright, so fluffy and white
Staring up at them, laying in long grass, what a delight.

Clouds drift and live a very long time,
Never following in their life, a straight line
Rain to storms, hot to cold, so many changes in the weather,
A cloud becomes old and heavy, where once it was light as a feather.

When they become heavy, a cloud will sink very low
Pieces of the cloud falls, we call it snow,
As the cloud, they come in all sizes and shapes,
Blanketing the earth, like one white untouched drape.

So next time you are shoveling, or playing in a fallen cloud
Think where it has traveled, it has been around,
Falling so gently, without making a sound
I love making snow angels, in a fallen cloud.

A Tree

A field, 160 years ago, grass is blowing in the breeze
A seedling takes root, proud to be amongst such beautiful trees,
It started small, and grew bigger with each day
Rain falls, sunshine, winds have blown it every which way.

But straight and tall, no matter the elements, always reaching to the sky
A family settles under him, a nice home, with a view for the eye,
Season after season, he grows and the family as well
Years pass, tree wonders, where are the old ones he can't tell.

The house abandoned, in his branches, he misses the children play
Houses going up all around, what used to be his field, is a street today.
Construction going on, no more trees, he stands alone
Cutting now through his branches, for satellite and phone.

Many birds, have called him home, no debt to be paid
A new friend, a squirrel within him, a home he has made,
Insects and disease spread through him, like their on parade
He starts to cry, as like all the others, he feels the saw blade.

Raindrop

In the cloud, part of him, home since he has been sane
His time has come, forming like a teardrop, he is called Rain,
Falls to the earth, by the wind a bit he is blown
Lands in a puddle, in a place unknown.

On the move, he's in the gutter and down a grate, to a sewer
Dirty, sick water everywhere, to them, he couldn't be any purer,
Staying with the current, he is now in a river
Flowing uncontrollably to the surface, a reflection of silver.

All he sees are smokestacks and factories, industrialization
Flushing sludge, taking over all the water, such pollution,
Empty of life this river, he is drifting with the tide
Sickness, trying to get him, staying pure, just a matter of time.

He is caught in a small stream
Resting gently in a motionless little bay, he spots a sunbeam,
He feels it's warmth, and rises back up to the clouds, but still
So many of his friends are sick, the cloud is now ill.

Part of him, the sickness, it be
Part of that pollution, you see,
Falling to the earth again, this time in pain
A new name, they call him, Acid Rain.

47

Dear Earth

From beyond the second star, not really that far
We write to you, wondering what kind of life, you are,
Is it a planet of junk, with all that debris, that surrounds your planet
A planet of war, with your own kind, you build weapons
    that will destroy it.

Your home, Earth you call it, amongst you race,
    many seek to control it
You damage your water, your air, your land,
    even the ozone layer around it,
You pollute yourselves, your home, the problem you just ignore it
You explore space, yet as a race, to us, a little barbaric.
A step ahead, yet backwards at the same time
When will your species learn, when you've crossed the line?

All together to better the race
Your planet, lives way too fast, who set that pace?
There are bets in the universe, on low long your planet will last,
I wrote this letter to you, hoping that someone,
    will do something fast.

You're the only planet, where all do not get along
Living in peace and harmony, this to all, even you earth, this belongs
Your planet so lush, and such a variety of life,
Taken for granted," They don't know how lucky they are,"
    I said to my wife.

PS : Live well, Earth...

48

Change

They say a leopard can't change his spots, this is not true
Especially, time for a change, if you are feeling blue,
A little rearrange at home, is good and a lot of fun
Trying a different food, except the same old thing on a bun.

Something new, something wild with a friend or two
Going for a walk, not bored, wondering what to do,
Joining a new club or trying a new sport
Getting out with you child, and building a fort.

A different place, or place to live, a new way
A new look, new style, a new life today,
A change is good sometimes, little or big
Learning a new dance, such as the Jig.

Try something new is great advice,
As log as it is nothing bad, that is bad advice,
But it may put a spark back into your life
Try something new, and take the wife.

Listen to the words you read before you today
Get out, live and love life, in your own special way,
In your life, before you turn another page
Try something new, try a change.

Life

Great, wonderful, magical, beautiful life, we love
Born today, with the grace of a dove,
Full of wonders in so many ways, each and every day
Never to be taken for granted in any given way.

To look at all as you did, years ago at the age of five
Amazement in your eye, at the sight of a beehive,
Buzzing around as we grow, life gets busier
In the woods, playing as a child, life gets easier.

As trees grow, time slowly ticks by
As a tree, our branches, the paths we take, always reaching for the sky,
Friends tend to come and go, with the turn of a page
Bringing new encounters, friends, memories, as we age.

Lucky enough to find the right mate
Never knew it until fate brought about that date,
Wanting a mate for the fairy tale
A home, children, a pet waving its tail.

Work, play, vacation, retire, life is very short
This I say to all of you, and I speak from my heart
Why rush and pass things by
To take in so much beauty, with your eye
Slow it down and see the beauty, that can be found,
All about you, like rain, a healing sound

Years pass by and you notice, changes in the bark
Looking in the mirror, first thing after dark,
Gone through life with the grace of a dove
Happy in knowing, once you found love.

Life fades, passes by, then away
Recharge your Spirit, and go play in the woods, today
Enjoy, have fun, dream, play and love life
Everyday while you're here, then everlasting life.

Music

Music, how it touches us all, to us all it belongs
Songwriters, singers, musicians, become one within a song,
Music like my writing, it comes from the heart
Like all other great works of art.

When you hear a song you like, you are bitten
A song becomes much more than a tune, that was written,
A song brings memories, along with it
This is an oldie, unexpected, on the radio, you hear it.

Crank it up, your concert with the band
Taken away, swept up by the beat, air guitar in hand
Whether at work, at home, in a car, anywhere
When you hear a song that carries a memory, instantly your there.

Feeling the groove, you start to move
First the foot, the leg, it's time to bust a move
It can help you exercise and look great
It will make you want to dance, when your on a date.

It can inspire and help create
Music like, Dream weaver, seemed to be written by fate,
It can help you relax, and free you from stress
For this, Dan Gibson's Solitudes, are the best
Go on and let the music play
And dance, the night away.

Imagination

Imagination, what a great part of creation,
Imagination, what a fascination,
Imagination, used in all inventions
Imagination, used in all books and movie creation,
Imagination, played a part, in our creation.

To different lands, sights that you may see
Different places, different person, you may be,
Imagination, everyone has used it, throughout our history
Some special effects, and imagination can become a reality.

Imagination, can be a mystery, like in a dream
Reading a book, your in it, imagination, can help it seem,
As a child, so much fun, no stress, used it regularly, day to day
No time now for imagination, or fun, some people say.

How does it work, where does it come from?
It's used in music, with an instrument and a drum,
It's used daily in almost every little thing
On stage you can sing, so much joy, imagination, can bring.

So creative, artistic, it can be
So that all can see,
That using imagination, is healthy, and not just for kids
Words of wisdom, anyone can use it, anytime, anywhere,
just for kicks.

Dreamers

One thing in common, we all have a dream
Even though as of yet, how far that dream may seem,
Try something new, you may have a creative talent
Don't let others tell you, that you ship has came and went.

Dreamers have made inventions, such as the phone
Some dreamer, this goes way back, invented the home,
Dreams, have written books, movies, and songs
A writer poet, this is where I belong.

Dream a dream, a dream weaver you are
Yes, even you, can reach for a star
You have a dream within your mind, that you die,
Let it be free, explore it, and go along for the ride.

You can dream a dream, and create, create, create,
Whether you are a senior citizen, to anyone,
    even those younger than eight,
Never, not believe in you, this is wrong
Everyone is a dreamer, you may write a hit song.

Explore your dream, you just never know
What to expect, you may dream, a Broadway show,
Whatever your dream may be
Share it with others, for the world to see.

Invent, some kind of invention
We are a marvelous part of creation,
Follow your dream, no matter, how far off it seems
Remember that one day, you started with a dream.

Dream a dream a dream weaver you are
I have chosen to create Echoes of a Shepard, as my star
Sharing a dream, dreamers, we are all the same
Be who you are, dare to dream, creation is found within your name.

Relaxing

Walking on a beach, a sunset, beauty not that rare
Lying in a hot bath, aromatherapy mix, if you dare
Close your eyes, it will sooth, it will calm,
Reducing stress, like a, mental stress balm.

Read a book, or go outside for a walk, that is a good start
A hot chocolate, a warm fire, nice and cozy, it'll warm the heart
The simple beauty, found in a tree,
Realize this, and of stress, you will be free
After the rain, taking in the smell
A foggy morning, you hear a church bell,

Cuddling, beside you your pet
Exercise, or work up a sweat
Putting on music and singing away
Adds flavor and fun to your day
We are a wonderful creation
Don't let them in, stress and frustration,

To relax, there available to us, is so much
It can come from a massage, and a gentle touch
So hear what I have to say,
Relaxing tools all around, go try one today.

The Children

Born, everything a wonder, everyday and everyway
Eyes see love, in parents eyes, they see beauty, as you lay
Innocence pure, hearts rejoice and sing,
A child, a gift from God, such a beautiful thing.

Years pass, learning what they see, and are taught
Sharing with them, so much joy, you ought
Early you start to hear their words of wisdom,
If you listen and talk with them, there will be magic in your kingdom.

Teachers to them, they are teachers to us
Some things, not worth, a lot of fuss
They love us and are blind to our faults
Going for a walk, a talk, to share a chocolate malt,
Always wanting to play and have fun
Good medicine, releasing your inner child, and playing under the sun.

They are our present, and our future
Seeing a child happy, our spirits, they nurture.
We were them not long ago
Remember this in your busy life, going to and fro.

Spending time with them is a gift and a luxury
Playing pirates in search of a golden treasury,
A respect for all on our earth
We should teach them from birth.

Cuddling at bedtime, to be taken away by dreams
Swinging like Spiderman, through the trees
We rise and shine, a new day begins
Wow, graduated high school, going into medicine,
Pride of a parent, nothing can compare
Except the memories, built together that we share.

Spiritual

It is around us everywhere, for us to nurture
God's creation and love, found within his works, in nature,
Forest, waterways, mountains, and meadows in the spring
These are the places, to pray, praise and sing.

Surrounded by his creations, this is how it should by
Not, in a man made, million dollar luxury
On top of a mountain, you'll see how peaceful it is in heaven
On his holy day, Sunday, the day of rest, day number seven.

He can be found within the Bible, his word
He can be found within the song of a bird,
Calm, like the voice of wilderness past, the common loon
Healing to the spirit, heard under a full moon
So creative was he, in the songs, sung by birds
A song sung from the heart, sung only to be heard,
Father in heaven, each night I pray
That balance, peace on earth, be found today.

Mother Earth

A better home for us all, God created for us, free
Full of different scenery, from sea to shining sea,
Healing water in a brook, a stream, or falling rain
Playing in her forests, brings the child back again.

Every sunrise, sunset, different, always there, faithful friend
Giving us warmth, beauty, and life all day, beginning to end,
Some seem to pollute it with no thought or care
Tears to my eyes, easy for them, hard for me to bare.

Mighty mountains, great valleys for all to enjoy
Vast wilderness can never be replaced by a toy,
No DVD, or videogame, can compare or match
To being outside, hiking, canoeing, or just playing catch.

All over the earth, medicine is found
Healing plants and roots all around,
Grass grows and the leaves fall to the ground
Each season with its own distinct sound,

Inspiring to a poets, writers and artist's imagination
Forever like the earth, a part of creation,
It touches us all in some simple way,
Love the earth it is our home today.

The Moon

Water changes, moves in and out, with the changing of the tide
Life sometimes may feel, like a rollercoaster ride,
All of us humans, are mostly water inside
The moon's cycle's, affects water, within us it resides.

What affect does the Moon, have on the water within our lives?
Does it affect us, as the changing of the tides?
Water, the moon, both have a healing touch
Beautiful creations like us, they affect us, as such.

A symbol of peace up in the sky
For all to see with their eyes,
To take in, and cleanse the spirit,
If the message, you choose to hear it.

So find what cycle of the moon, is best for you
Between the cycle's, you'll notice differences, this is so true.
Without the moon, life would be blue
Who is the man in the moon? Really who?

The same man who made all of creation
We made it to the moon, with imagination and determination,
To the earth, our moon seems to belong
So beautiful the moon, in PoeArtry, and song.

You have protected us from Asteroids, and meteor showers
You have taken many hits for us, and we send you no flowers,
Like a knight in armor, and so much more, is our moon
Suspended in space, a floating balloon

Look to the moon, beauty abound
Pearl white, gleaming, sometimes perfectly round,
Been with us all throughout history
In days of not long ago, the moon was a mystery.

Now to the moon, we seek to go no more,
We have already, opened that door,
Progress, now reach to the planets and stars,
Time to focus on our home, not someplace far.

The Storm

I'm scared, high wind, hard rain, a loud flash, thunder echo
Lightning hit the earth as I lay upon my pillow,
Heart beats faster, as I pace the floor
Yellow sky, Tornado watch, how much more.

Howling winds, send the rain, pounding on the window pane
In the house alone, power out, all but going into shock, I refrain,
My instincts tell me, that is not good
I'm glad I'm in the house, not hiking in the woods.

To my ears, it sounds like the end of the world
All of a sudden, I feel a little cold,
Very dark and grey now, I close my eyes
Thunder echoes, across the sky.

I'm so nervous, I'm so tense, I can't sit, I can't rest
From losing it altogether, I'm doing my best,
What was that? door opens, my pets are home
They'll protect me, now The Storm, seems more calm.

Chipmunk

On a trail, in a northern forest, one day
Came upon a second path, let's go this way,
My brother, a friend and I, enjoying the scene
A hawk soars above us, eyes so keen.
Birds are singing all around
In the trees, look hard, they can be found,
Sharing the day in nature, just us three
We stop, amazed at the size of that bee.

What size, oh, he or she could give a nasty sting
Attracted to the shine of my friends ring,
Continuing on, after sharing a good laugh,
Thinking, this is such a beautiful path.
A Chipmunk ran across the path, stopped to have a look,
Looking at us, as if caught on a hook,
Kneeling down to his level, such peace in his eye,
I started singing softly to him or her, under a blue sky.

All three of us, the chipmunk, wondering what we are,
Sat there calmly, listening, as if admiring a star,
Enjoyed our song, we knew he said," Thank you"
This was incredible to do, a story that is true,
We wished him well, and continued on our way,
A memory that will be with me forever, it will stay,
I felt so alive to be so, free
I wonder if the chipmunk, even remembers me.

The Microwave Syndrome

In today's fast rabbit paced world, we must slow down,
Everyone rushing, on foot, in car, around town,
Passing by so much medicine, for their spirit, with their eyes,
We rush out the door, speeding even on our good byes,
Life is short, yet we rush through it,
No time, "Really" to enjoy it,
Drive thru's, instant dinner's, it's all on the go today,
With the internet, the world just got smaller, in some way.

The microwave syndrome, who set this pace?
Why do we think, we are always in a race?
So much stress, cramping so much, in so little time,
The microwave syndrome, a sign, that we are almost crossing the line,
Around the globe, you can see its effects,
Dreamers like me, this disease, we can detect,
Quick fix's, marriage, it affects all,
On a busy day you can see it, just go to the mall.

If you have it, then try to slow yourself down,
It is not good for your health, rushing around town,
Find time for you, and life too,
Caught up in the pace, you feel trapped, like in a zoo,
But, you are not trapped, the cure, is free will,
Be original to escape it, you do not need to take a pill,
Get out in the woods and play today,
Listen to my words, and what they have to say.

Slow it down, you'll notice a change right away,
Better coping skills, a slower pace, needed each day,
Not so much flooding your mind,
Life is short, you can slow it down, time,
Be weary of the microwave syndrome,
No one knows how it got here, or where it comes from,
One thing I know is, that it is not for me,
I like spending time, just sitting under a tree.

No time for the children, what then will our future, have to say,
Release your inner child, get out in life and play today,
Slow it down in life, and take a look,
Relax, time for you to pick up a book,
Recharge your Spirit, a book worth the look, and so much more,
Escape the microwave syndrome, open the door,
Slow down the pace, and we will win the race,
Working together, sharing this planet, we are the Earth race,
Break free, this will bring a smile to your face,
If we all are smiling, then we will win the race.

Friend of a Friend's, Friend

There's a girl I know, so nice and that's a fact,
Why is she with him, what does she see in that,
He doesn't treat her nice, that is so bad,
Hit's her, doesn't think twice, that is so sad.

If with her for just a bit, I'd show her what it is, to feel love,
She walks in beauty with the grace of a dove,
So soft she'd be, one hour, to show her what love can be,
To be with me, so magical together, she would see,
Even if she chose to be a friend, and not a lover,
I'd still be friends with her, while with another,
But so much better that girl deserves,
If only she could get up the nerves

To leave a man, who does not see,
Her true beauty, and what she could be,
I could love her so good, I would touch her heart,
If only she would leave him, a fresh new start.

We were friends once, but after what I saw, he is not a friend for me,
I wish you would listen to what I have to say, so much better, it would be,
You have so many options girl, even though, it may not seem,
A better life awaits you, awaken your dreams.

Woke up this morning, the TV, I turned on,
In anger a man shot a woman, it was you, now your gone,
I cry, as I think, to what may have been,
With us together, a future, now just a dream,
For any other, my words they hear,
Don't be afraid to interfere,
You never know, you may just save a life,
That life you save, may one day be your wife.

Friend

Some friends in life may come and go, or you just outgrow,
In memory, friends, always they'll be, reminded, watching a old show,
New ones through life, I am sure you will meet,
You never know what life, has in store, for a treat.

A work or vacation, some friendships, you do not want to end,
In time a friend may become, a best friend,
To talk, share and so much more,
To help when your sick, or down, that is what a friend is for.

Sometimes you may disagree, and not see eye to eye,
A friendship that is endless, will see the problem pass by,
Not causing hurt, sadness, or pain,
It is fun walking with a friend, in the rain,

Some, as kids we would climb a tree,
Some true as glue, for all to see,
Play the lone ranger, like a raccoon in a mask,
For a friend, you really, don't even have to ask,
In life a true friend, is hard to find, too few,
You do many things together, dark skies or blue,
A friend, never take one for granted, this is so true,
Can't be replaced, a friend who is a friend, as true as glue.

Campfire

Sitting and forming a circle, called the campfire ring,
Watch the fire, the flames dance and sing,
The crackling and the sound of the wood,
Enhanced by a story, marshmallows, being as it should.

Ghost stories, spooky tales, told in the mystery of night,
As a child, all in fun, to give a good fright,
Reflections of fairies trying to catch the light,
Legends of Bears, Bigfoot and other creatures of the night,

The feeling of having a fire under the night sky,
Sharing it with a lover, puts a twinkle, in both your eyes,
Cuddling by a fire, two can become one,
Calmed by the fire, a good night's sleep, till the rising of the sun,

Out in the woods, by a stream, the warmth on your face,
You walk away, look back, you realize, your caught up in the race,
The campfire, gives you a break anytime of the week,
With a campfire, peace and solitude, is what I seek.

It's all over, check twice, making sure it is all out,
Starting a forest fire, is not what I am about,
The good old fashioned campfire,
Your healing mood, I desire.

Writers of Books

Writers they can touch us and make us cry,
They have left us sometimes, asking why?
In another land, someone else you can be,
A pirate, in search of a treasure, on the open sea.

They write thrillers, romance, suspense, and mystery,
Many a great writer, have been discover, throughout history,
So creative with their way with words,
It can become music, once read aloud and heard.

Bookstores, Libraries, are the entrance way to far off lands,
Books of science fiction to westerns, with guns or light sabers, in hands,
We care and despise, some of the characters,
We turn the pages, we becomes the page masters.

Classics found like Treasure Island, to the Lord of the Rings,
To masterpieces as Recharge your Spirit, and the Sting,
From gangsters, like Al Capone,
To monsters, that will scare you, to the bone.

Something for everyone, writer's share,
A hand written poem, may show one, that you care,
UFO s, alien life, to civilizations gone,
Star trek, adventures in space with the Klingon.

Writers like Mark Norris to Terry Brooks,
Show us their dreams, in their books,
When was the last time, you picked up a book,
Visit a bookstore, and have a look.

Fisherman Dave

We'd play, hike, have fun, at Ojibway and Jackson Park
Always had laughs, even when it was bedtime, after dark,
Sometimes, you would read me, your ill-bred, a story as I fell asleep,
Sometimes as a big brother, by accident, you would make me weep,

Brothers forever, always so much fun,
Just being together, under the sun,
Roller-skating, at school, my big bro fisherman Dave, would protect me,
You, Kevin, and I, three brothers, soon we became we.

Years we age, differences, but brothers we stay,
How we love to fish, on a quiet northern bay,
Now with a wife and son, and me the same, of my own,
King of the mountain, I was never able to knock you off that throne.

It is always nice to visit you at home,
Love in a small way, is always shown,
A great teacher to me, in so many ways,
A drunk driver, has taken fisherman Dave's life away, the other day,
Now on a mountain, I miss him, in photos and my memory,

With us, your wife, your son of ten years, so much history,
My brother is in peace up in heaven,
He is a part of everything now, says my other brother, Kevin,
He is in the beauty, found in the little flower eagle, the hummingbird,
He is now in a song, once it is heard.

My big bro, fisherman Dave, I love and miss you,
You were a great friend, person, this is so true,
We never even had the chance to say good bye,
I know that you do not want to see, us cry.

But for love, our hearts, must let it out, with emotion and tears,
We shared so much in your short 40 years,
Please, do not drink and drive, a life or two, or more, you may save,
Again a teacher, my big brother Fisherman Dave.

Love you brother,
For you David, go #24, and fish on.
In loving memory of "David Stuart Norris"
For Tyler, and all of his family.

My Son and I

With my son playing, so much fun under the sun,
Hockey, football, together as we run,
On a journey, on a mission to save the world, or just on a hike,
Spending time with him, like learning to ride a bike.

In a meadow we fly a kite,
Lunch, time for a little bite,
Wrestling, playing on the bed,
Ouch, he accidentally, kicked me in the head.

Shoveling or playing in a fallen cloud, that we call snow,
Such good medicine, I never say no,
In the fall, jumping in a pile of leaves,
In the mud, covered from head to toe, even our sleeves.

Going for a walk in the day or night, anytime of the week,
To games like PS2, and old ones like, Hide and Seek,
For one day, no time for me, he'll have to spend
Friends, girls, Ill be lucky to see him on the weekend..

Playing like a child, you'll see how healthy it can be,
We are cowboys, partners, friends, together, we are we,
This is how it should be,
Spending time in nature, exploring or climbing a tree.

I love him with all my heart,
I have, right from the start,
Playing under the blue sky, and sun,
My son and I, we are one.

The Anniversary

On a first name basis, only at first, then to babe, my sweet,
When I met you, I knew I was in for a treat,
One year passed, it seems like just yesterday, we just met,
In love now, moving in together, time for a pet.

Many, end in divorce, by this time,
In court, what is yours, is now mine,
We've made it through some stormy weather,
Still a kiss from you, I'm as light as a feather,
Still together, in so much we share,
What great news, a child, you now bare,
Such love these days, is rare,
Sometimes you catch me looking at you, in a stare.

To cuddle wuddle in bed, a perfect fit,
Watching TV, all sqoozy woozy, as we sit,
Today I realize, we have come a long way,
Kids, have left for college today,
Even though 74 years of age, I love you still, the same way,
I wish we could climb up to the old tree fort, and make out today.

How long since we hugged, seems like forever, you've been gone,
I've never forgotten, each day I listen to our song,
The house so quiet with you, not around,
I always turned to you, when something could not be found,

Time, how some things change,
In the book of love, for us, they should write a new page,
How long ago since we heard those words, "You two should marry."
I've always loved you, Babe, my sweet, Happy Anniversary.

Tia

I saw her, a good friend, I knew she and I would be,
Her and I, it was fate, a part of the family, she will be,
All cuddly, shiny, black and gold,
My sweetie rottwieller, so happy, to me, she was sold.

A true companion, a friend better than most,
She'd wait for me, like I was the world's greatest host,
To play ball, wrestle, or just lay down with you, on the ground,
Sounded like a grizzly bear, how I loved her sound.

Seeing any sign of skin, was a invitation to lick, like I am candy,
Dog hair everywhere, every little nook and cranny,
She loved to eat, no matter what it was,
Walking by, I'd spot her, I'd stop and cuddle her, just because.

The wave of her body, as she would say hello,
Up on the couch, she was happier, than a kid with Jell-O,
We traveled her, there, and everywhere,
Always safe, I'm glad we never ran into a bear.

To my life, my wife and child, you brought us so much joy,
A stuffed little yellow duck, was her favorite toy,
A half of a tennis ball, was gold to your eye,
Bags in our hands, so excited, what did they buy?

My sweetie rottwieller girl, we will miss you,
When we buried her, a eagle, landed in the tree branch above,
this is true,
Thank you girl for all, no matter the mood or the weather,
We shared 14 years, of a fun filled, happy life together.

Stress

S- Stress {causes}
T- Trouble within {which}
R- Reduces our immune system {eventually}
E- Enters our being {causing}
S- Slow down in productivity, creativity, and energy {leading to}
S- Stretches our balance within, Shortens our lives.

W- Why
O- Overthink
R- Reasons and/or
R- Responses
Y- You are not in control of.

Stress can make your sacred circle, quite a mess
Sometimes, you can't take it, you've given it your best,
Relax, breathe deep, take some time for yourself
This is for you and your health,
Wherever you are, you can close your eyes
Silent your thoughts, let the trouble pass you by,
Do not let the Stress seed within
Taking root, frustration will begin.

This may seem hard, but you are in control
Keep life simple, happy, too much stress, will take its toll,
Drift with the wind, ride the tide, go with the flow
Don't get flustered or lose control, then emotions blow,
Stay calm, the situation, it is not worth is
Stress intake, like smoking, it is a bad habit
With you, stress and worry, will not have their way
No stress, start to smile, see how much better, you will feel today.

Addiction

It's all around the world, people have it, in every nation
Smoking, gambling, alcohol, drugs, there are many forms of addiction,
Our loved ones, friends, strangers, for all we should care
If someone has an addiction, to them, life is not fair,
It has ruined families, marriages, and destroyed lives
It has made some steal, from their loved ones, even their wives,
Some turn to crime, to support their habit
On the street, living in fear, like a wild rabbit.

Too much time, many, wasted away
How many lives will be ruined, today,
A friend as true as glue
To help them see, to help them through,
It is like, to many, a game they play
A high they cannot get any other way,
Time to stop, even in moderation, today
Just say No, the youth of today, can say.

Some don't even see that what they do is a sin
With an addiction, they must believe, they can quit and win,
Patience, Love, and Understanding
Will help anyone through anything,
So if you know one, with any kind of addiction
Show them this with time and determination,
They are still a beautiful part of creation
Show them that life is the fascination.

Prescription of Medicine
Recharge Your Spirit

An act of kindness or love can go a long way
Show these to a friend, or anyone today
Look at all the beauty, it is around
Relax, play, have fun and find your sound,
A healing sound, as water can help you relax
Medicine for the mind, body, and spirit, in my book, these are the facts.

Look at things from a different angle, or try something new
Be with a loved one, under a sky of blue
A simple hello, good day to you
Random acts of kindness, too few,
A kind word, gentleness, to handle a stressful situation
Help someone with love, escape an addiction,
Eat healthy foods, healthy drinks like water or five alive
Don't drink and drive, most want to stay alive.

Think of others, not just yourself
These things and much more, are so good for your health,
Words of wisdom, your prescription for each day
Recharge your Spirit, I know it will help, in some small way,
On a global scale, this would be so nice
A prescription, to do per day, twice,
Peace on earth, would spread across the land
One at a time, like me, pen in hand...

Recharge your Spirit, a prescription you should start
Immediately you will feel it touch your heart,
From mine to yours, to another it will travel
A prescription, as the ripple, will become as popular as gravol,
For a better life, earth, this prescription must be taken
From where we are heading, we must awaken
Love yourself, each other, and all our relations
Each one of us, is an incredible piece of creation.

A Snail

Sit back, curl up, a tea, reading blanket, and listen to my tale
Of a great journey in my life, 4 hours, I spent with a snail,
On a hike, a root, all moss covered, under a tree, I stopped for a rest
Discovering that I was not alone, I thought my patience, to test.

A forest snail, traveling somewhere, very slow
Carrying his home on his back, rather than in tow,
Coming up to twigs and leaves, a giant obstacle to overcome
He seems to stop, but then straight he presses on, until the obstacle is done.

Almost 3 hours work, so huge to him, yet so small to me
What a lesson, what a teacher, how wise a snail can be,
I wonder if he is even proud of what he has done
When I asked him, no answer, did come.

Time seems so insignificant, to him, no bother
On a mission it seems, some adventure, maybe to find another,
I decide to get up and continue on my way
Good bye to him, and I wondered, where his journey ended that day.

Humane Society

Humane Society, what a great job, these people do
Rescue heroes for the animals, sometimes us, as well too,
Cruelty to animals should be extinct, and not exist
To a loving animal, how can someone raise a fist,

They care for the animal, help it find a good home
Love, play, attention, not left on a chain, with a bone,
A variety of animals, if you walk in, you will see
All wanting to be loved, by someone, for free.

Free to be the pet, you need them to be
Some eventually taught to help the blind see,
You walk in, to home, you'd like to take them all
Sitting in a room full of puppies or cats, you'll have a ball.

And if by chance you choose one, to be with you
If you show it love, you get it back ten fold, this is so true,
So visit your local humane society, and see what you see
You may just meet your best friend, to be.

The Eagle

So proud, so wild and free, majestic, unstopped by gravity
To be this way forever, is your destiny,
To fly, how wonderful that must be
Living in balance, peace and harmony.

Ancient presence, suspended effortlessly in space
Moving through the air, riding the winds, with such grace,
Eyes that can see deeper than thought
Through the eagle, legends are taught.

The eagle has something to teach us all
So inspiring as the colors in the fall,
A master of the four winds
Pure, unchanged in time, free from sin.

A symbol of pride and freedom to so many
So famous, yet you own not a penny,
To feel the wind, under my wings and to feel that free
Time would stand still, and that time, would always be.

The Eagle, a apart of creation for us to see
How God works is always a mystery,
But with the eagle, and the beauty, found in creation
I know that God was happy, with his imagination.

What Can It Be?

It is as old as time itself, an ageless wonder
For it's solitude and beauty, we grow fonder,
In the hearts of all, in all countries and races
Many who enjoy it, have differences, like their faces,
We use it in so many ways, we are using it today
Some call it home, still living there today
When you near one, your troubles seem, to fade away.

Peace and harmony, medicine, within one can be found
In one near one, near water, what a beautiful sound,
Some seem to pollute it with no care or thought
To leave it, as we find it, we ought.

God, creation, faith, are found within it
Tranquility, solitude, are contained within it
Lessons, worth all the wisdom of our schools, can be found within it,
Comfortable, when your within it, you start to embrace it.

You'll find it, just as simple as going for a walk
With a friend, sharing good times and talk,
So many answers, within one can be found
Inspiring artists throughout history, be still in one, listen to the sound.

What can it be? You are within a {oetsrf }

The Fountain of Youth
It Has Been Discovered!

Many have gone in search for, the fountain of youth
It doesn't exist, it is within each of us, this is the truth,
Ponce de Leon, living free, an explorer on the open sea
Youth, found in a pool of water, it is not to be,
Our existence, our life, short, on the scale of time
As adults, youth found in a cream, they'll stand in line,
In a bottle we hear that wrinkles will fade
They are a sign of wisdom, that comes with age.

For within us all is a child wanting to play
When was the last time, you allowed yourself, to play all day,
Releasing your inner child, is good medicine, that's the truth
Found within each of us, seek, there it is, the fountain of youth,
Age is of time, pay it no matter, with age, time goes by
Read each word, take them in deep, with your eye
You are as young as you want to feel, both you and I.

So go play, explore in the woods, today
Once you find the fountain of youth, within, it will always stay
Hurry up, get out there, all it takes is, fun and play
It is that simple, this, is what I say
Try it, and you'll find it today.

Shirley Temple

Curly top, you little bundle of joy
To watch her movie, I'd put away my favorite toy,
Get home from church, in time, for the Sunday matinee
Littlest Rebel, Wee Willie Winkie, which one will be, today

At the time black and white TV, was not bother
Then they made the bluebird, and in color,
The best in the business, don't you agree
A finer child actress or actor, you'll never see.

She danced and sang, played her part like a pro
Brought out emotions, from me to my big bro's
Thoughts of yesterday, as I think of her today
How she made me feel, still does, to this day, in her special way.

I think of Heidi, and her good ol'"Granpa
The best of her films that I ever saw
She touched us all, right from the start
Forever and ever, she will be in our hearts.

Thank you Shirley Temple for the memories
Forever you are a part of movie history,
A true classic, a hall of famer, an all time great
All by the time, she reached the age of eight.

Oprah

Oprah Winfrey, the greatest TV host of all time
Just for a chance to meet her, people stand in line,
A host, that truly shares and cares
Looking good in anything she wears.

You go girl, you dared to dream
The Color Purple, how long ago it must seem,
You've come so far, since your start
Oprah truly cares from the heart.

A great friend, an honor, that would be
With Oprah, for anyone, including me,
Her shows touch us like no other, by far
Oprah shines, as one of the brightest stars.

With soft eyes, a smile that captures the sun
Feel good girl, about all that you have done,
She'd walk a mile to hold a empty hand
Oprah for president, across the land.

All in all, she is just like you and I
Shows us all, to reach for the sky,
An inspiration to so many
Following in her footsteps, shows as Montel, to Jenny.

But Oprah, the real, original deal
Into many lives, she brings a magical feel
Thank you Oprah, from the world to me
For dreaming a dream, that came to be.

Essence of the Cowboy

Thunder echoed through the mountains
Wind, as a wolf howled across the ranchland,
Cattle, horses raised their heads, uncertain
For the birth of a rare breed, a cowboy was at hand.

From birth he is taught the code, eyes at attention
A bond with nature, he is a part of creation
His best friend, his soul mat, a horse named, Tradition.

In his cowboy hat, on the trail
Fixing fences, a "yeeeehaw", his familiar wail,
Breaking horses and caring for the flock
Never knowing the time on the clock.

He rides these hills seldom seen
You may catch a glimpse of him, in a moonbeam,
Poetic as moonlight, on fresh fallen cloud, we call snow
Part of history, the cowboy will never go
When your in need of help, he'll never say no
His horse and him, become one on the go.

Last of a rare breed, battling the elements
Riding trails for over 100 years
May the circle continue for the cowboy.

Pride is a part of his life
Wanting a cowgirl for his wife,
To have some little cow folk of their own
The circle completed for one more go around.

A Message

Throughout my PoeArtry, a message sent from me to you
Even though, caught in the rat race, feeling part of the zoo,
A message sent, a message needed to be heard
Over and over again, so much, within a song sung by a little bird
Pollution, war, money, greed, from history, a warning sign to heed
Do not stress within to take root, to take seed,
Have faith, read the bible, believe in God and heaven above
Peace on earth, the whole circle, we all need love.

Dream a dream, play as a child
Go for a hike, camp, spend time in the wild,
Teach the children, a respect for all to share
The fate of our future, our earth, in their hands we must care,
Enjoy so much, all this great world has to offer
Why only in disasters, do we pull together,
Learning from history, progressing this far
Then let us, it's time to put a stop to war.

The love of a wife, a husband, pets and children
Read a good book, perhaps one called, Animal Medicine,
Memories of loved ones, days of old, never go away
Movies are great, cuddle up, and watch one today,
Old fashioned guy, a cowboy I am, this is true
Wild crazy, full of passion, romance, a friend, true as glue,
Something always a mystery, each life is a story, each is a book
Creative within you may be, PoeArtry, worth the look.

Feel great and love who you are
A campfire, a story, a song, a night under a star,
Take car, love a pet, a best friend, they'll always be
Unconditional love, a rare sight to see
The elements of life, can seem like the "Storm"
Listen to music, jam, or go fishing with a worm
Be thankful for what you have, life is great
Go to a concert, car race, NFL game, feeling groovy going in the gate.

Take time to enjoy a sunrise, or a tranquil sunset
Go for a bike, canoe ride, go to the beach and get wet,
Slow down life, between the risings of the moon
Try something new, maybe fly in a big balloon,
Knowledge is of the past, wisdom for the future
A flower, our spirits, they nurture
Share love and love one another
Volunteer, be a big sister, or a big brother.

Merry Christmas mindset, all through the happy new year
Peace on earth, joy to the world, remember the "Deer",
Let it be like this every day of the week
Peace, solitude, love all you seek,
Let good intent, good meaning be in all I do, in all I say
Sing in life, like the Loons on Echo bay,
I wish you all well, as you continue on your journey today
I hope you get the message sent, and it helps you, in some way.

Messages Sent

Many Messages sent, many different ways,
For anyone who hears, what dreamers, have to say.
Disney in so many ways, has touched the children
As well as the parents, adults, men and women.

Pocahontas, Spirit, to Brother Bear,
The Lion King, Dinosaur, with the Circle of Life, a song for you to hear.
With a cartoon, a story, and songs with deep meaning,
Intended for the future, to be healing.

To musicians as well like, Pink Floyd and the Wall
United they sing "Feed the World", should be sung by all,
To Alabama's," Pass it on down" to songs as "If a Tree falls",
For John Lennon's "Imagine", a dreamer, he touched us all.

Songs that sing about truth as "I'll Fly Away" by Jars of Clay,
      to many more,
Even Ozzy Ozbourne, in the song Dreamer, what next is in store?
Recharge your Spirit, by Mark A Norris, will open that door,
Within his book, not just words, but much, much more.

Messages sent in many different ways
Another, watching Oprah today,
All different ways the message is sent, still it remains the same,
To touch all on the earth, even those that have fame.

Sharing this planet, different we are, yet the same
For its fate and ours, interwoven, the circle, we are to blame,
Peace on Earth, we are one, we are the Earth race,
We must slow down our pace.
The message, will keep being inspired, by God, from above,
Until we choose to, listen, and live, in peace, harmony and love.

Health Is Inner Peace #1

Every once in a while we seem to try to set ourselves apart in a quiet, restful, and peaceful place. This vacation to get away usually consists of getting back to nature and the beauty of creation. Humankind is the only part of creation that has chosen to live away from the natural world. We return on our vacation, because of the spiritual connection that we have with Creation, it bonds us.

Stress, anxiety and the negative energies enter our being, because we allow the seed to rest in the soil of our minds. To grow roots within us, causing aches, pain, and in some cases, serious illness, that can be fatal. Many feel this coming on due to all the fun stuff, that life brings into our paths. A lot of this stems from everything in our lives being built around speed. The Microwave Syndrome of today's fast, rabbit paced world. Why must we over speed in everything such as driving, breakfasts, lunches, dinners and family quality time.

We watch our diets and exercise for our outward appearance, but do we spend any time working out the spirit of kindness within. True beauty, true health, starts from within, this should be our #1 concern for overall health, there has to be balance with mind, body and spirit.

Listen to the song of a bird it is uplifting, teaching us that what comes from our voice, should be in beauty and from the heart. Allow only positive and beautiful energy in and out of yourself.

This is so important today, there is such a high amount of negative energies, polluting the are we breathe, the water we drink, the earth we live on, the shy above us, the workplace, bills, it is all around us on a daily basis. Making personal balance, more important than ever before. Awaken you Spirit, be at peace and seek the grace of our great Creator.

Humankind has grown so much intellectually, scientifically with the focus being that of technology and progress, to the point that we have affected everything around us. But, yet spiritually we have grown very little, We have lessoned spiritual talk, sharing, and caring for our fellow man, where it has slowed the growth with ourselves, and our relationship to God. We seem to be caught up in a world where the main focus, is on outward appearance or top name brand expensive, materialistic things. To what others think of us, how we compare to others, this influences our lives as it harbors many negative energy patterns, within ones spirit, and the body, which will affect health and lifestyle.

Finding the quiet of the pure mind is not as common as once it may have been. Look at all the alternative medicines that have come about in the last decade. Yet meditation prayer, is as old as time, all the great people of our history, used it in one form or another. Yet, it has become forgotten. This is where you will find, what has mostly been explained as calm and consistent light within, channel your power from here, I call it my spirit.

We must listen with openness, when we fear what we do not understand. We must learn to be open to messages being sent from within and without. From all that surrounds us in life, the plants, animals, trees, every little thing, for the generous and creative ways people enter our lives.

Listen to the whispers within. It is time for the unity of the human race, to become the earth race, under God.

This will happen as more and more people find Jesus and inner peace. Instill these values throughout life's journey. This gentle respect for one another and all of creation must come for the sake of our children's children.

98

Listen to the song of water, and hear what it has to say to you. Don't wait for an actual voice; you'll be there for a long time. (ha,ha,ha,). But a soothing sound will enter your ear that is for sure.

Listen to a tree as the wind blows through its branches, and hear what the wise one has to say. Sit out in the rain, or play in the mud, are words of wisdom. Release your inner self; don't let cobwebs cloud your dreams, from you. Spend time in creativity, prayer and spiritual exercise.

Find that deep relaxation state of being let God's love inner light shine through; this is the path to inner peace. With inner peace, a balanced diet, exercise, this is the trail to true health. Seek guidance within, where all the answers lie, where all great ideas are born, we truly are a beautiful part of creation, and we should act like that. Live in harmony, walk softly in life, God bless, and journey well.
Mark A Norris

Health Is Inner Peace #2

It is almost that time of year again, that winter wonderland, in the mountains where I live.

The forests covered in a blanket of fresh fallen cloud, (we call snow), under the blue light of the full moon. Such beauty and wonder to enter our sense. One of the most magical settings, are when I hear about groups of people who gather to self heal, to reflect, to help each other, within silence and prayer. A gathering of friends, doing this is a great health thing, for mind, body and spirit. Embracing our neighbor is good medicine for you.

What good ripples to put out across space and time. Always be attentive to what you are sending out, as in time when they return to you, you want them to be carrying positive energy back your way.

Within harmony with nature, are ripples that will spread out to your work and personal lives.

Around yourself, like the beaver teaches us to build a dam. As the Beaver build your dam against stress, worry, frustration, and all the negative energies that may come your way. Simply by using sticks and logs, of fun, love, and of memories new and old. If by chance the water of negative lake rises to high against your dam, you'll be aware, and then you can reinforce it with the strongest log of all, a simple smile, filled with love and faith. The dam is the first part of stopping stress, by helping you, become aware, when the water of stress lake is rising to high, identification, before it can enter your spirit.

Walking in balance with God is pure light in darkness. Black is color, as it is the color that surrounds you when you are at a most peaceful state, sleep. In silence or to pleasant sounds we search this color in meditational prayer and reflection, and many of us look good wearing black. To be a negative, you have to allow it within the soil of your mind, to your spirit.

In a world where the old ways of life are slowly disappearing, it is important to walk in balance with the new day, but with old time values. Live a health life starting from deep within, then the ripples will spread out to the bones, the muscles, organs and bloodstream, as the body will always follow the leader, the spirit.

By stopping stress within to take seed in the soil of your mind, your lawn will be free of stress weed, and now weeds allows for maximum growth within the lawn of your mind. The key to peace is in all our hearts, open the door, and you will find Jesus. We neglect our true inner spirit where so much lies in a dormant state. Even our athletes are discovering the power of meditation and reflection. For the individual, couple, family, group, town, city, country, and global health, God is the key.

Look at what is best, for the whole. All our answers lie in each of our pasts, like they say, knowledge is of the past, wisdom is the future. Where one's footsteps have been in life become familiar and routine, but you can turn them into a healthy ritual, of fun. Embrace each footstep in life, with beauty and love for all things. This is the trail to true health, as true beauty starts within. We are all part of the web of life. Take care of your personal web. Because what happens to one strand, soon spreads to the whole web if not mended. If the center of your web is at inner peace with God, then all will be at peace.

I look at the earth and the forests and smile, in turn they smile back. As I try to be a reflection of all the beauty that I see in creation. What is healthy living, it is listening to the song sung by crickets, it is in the feeling of being barefoot in the cool sand, it is dancing on a mountain top, it is when one sits and watches the sunset, and the moon rise, to awake with the rising of the sun. It is in the spirit of all things.

God bless and good journeys...

From Me to You

Well here we are, from me to you. Thank you for sharing my dream with me. I hope that you have enjoyed yourself and that I have in some small way, touched your life. Then this book, has accomplished what it was written for. On top of a mountain, this is what I heard, in a song, sung by a little bird. My writing poured out of me, using poetic rhyme, that I call PoeArtry. I have had a difficult time trying to decide which one is my favorite. But, after much thought, it would have to be "Little Bird", a very close second would be, "Invisible". What are yours?

I have enjoyed each letter as I printed them, on paper. They have flowed through me with love, and faith in God above. My dream I pray will come true, and if you are reading this, then my dream has come to be. This is the poetic art found within my PoeArtry. Maybe you will try something new, creative, you just never know where your dream, may take you.

It was written for you right from the start, as I wrote, from one spirit to another. Out in nature we belong, as the bird, sing from your heart a song of peaceful beauty. As children, play all through life, these are words of wisdom, as this book is for our future.

I have enjoyed our little journey together through some magical pages. If ever we meet I hope we will say, "Hello and good day to you". But for now we have come to the end, but there is one more thing that I would like to say to you. Have faith, dream, be kind to one another, love and seek the grace of our great creator, God. Spend time in nature, his creations, read the Bible, and listen to the voice of truth, to the whispers within...

Dear Reader,

I would like to hear your thoughts on my little book, and how it may have touched your life, or someone you care about. I believe that much can be said, without a lot of words, as much, can be learned within silence. Please include which one you liked the most.

Help the Ripple along, it's journey to the four directions of our planet. Spread good echoes on the winds of grace. You may decide to give copies of this book as gifts, to family, and friends. The gift of a healthier existence for one, to the world. From my heart, to yours, to another's, let the echoes continue...

My next book is in the making, my friends, but until then, I look forward to hearing from all of you.

If by chance you would like to contact me for business reasons, such as, a speaker, for your church, a spiritual or health conference. Or for TV, or for Radio, you can also reach me at the email address below.

Contact Mark A Norris, at

Email; mnpoeartry@hotmail.com

Till next time,

God bless and good journeys, my friends...

Live in the light, abide in love, and let the circle of goodness continue...

Back to the Illusion, now..

Recharge Your Spirit
Echoes of a Shepherd

Open your heart, with a book unlike any other. Explore it, set it free and prepare for the memory, of a lifetime. From the forests, comes a sunrise for a cloudy world. Mark touches deep beyond the eye with peaceful grace to refresh life, Recharge your Spirit.

A magical journey through beautifully written pages, take you on a mystical transformation to inspire kindness, care and love. With discoveries such as the Microwave Syndrome, and the Elevator Disease, Mark's unique down to earth philosophy, reawakens the senses.

A rainbow of words, a fountain of youth in wisdom, a waterfall of healing to the spirit, Mark believes that each one of us can make a difference.

Every once in a while a writer will bloom, blessed with a gift to leave echoes within the reader.

Mark A Norris is such a writer.

Printed in the United States
75507LV00002BA/4-69